★ ★

FRONTIERSMEN OF AMERICA

Francis Marion

SWAMP FOX

MATTHEW G. GRANT

Illustrated by John Keely and Dick Brude

GALLERY OF GREAT AMERICANS SERIES

★ ★

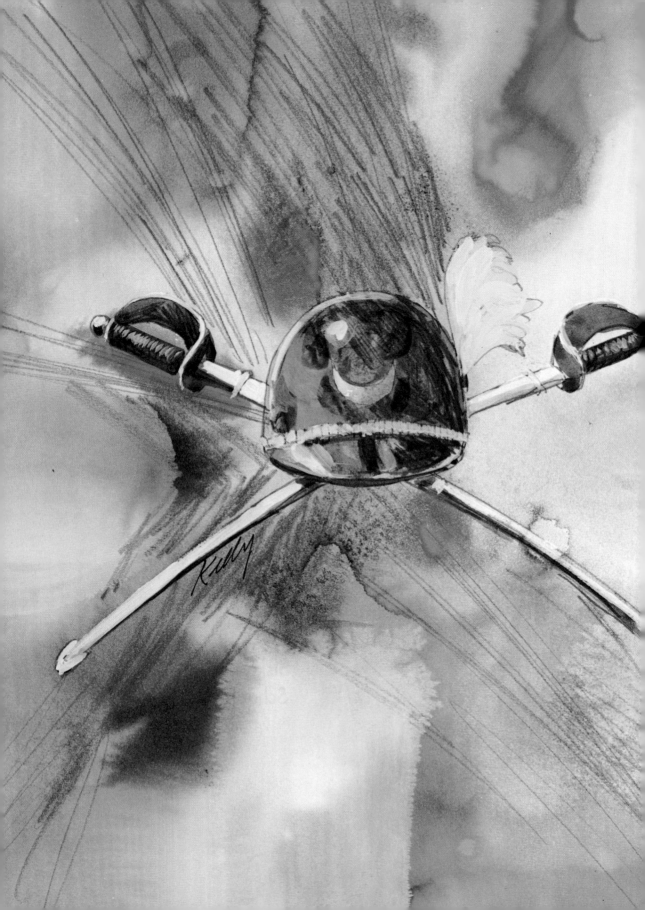

Francis
Marion

SWAMP FOX

Library of Congress Number: 73-10061   ISBN: 0-87191-257-0

Published by Creative Education, Mankato, Minnesota 56001
Distributed by Childrens Press, 1224 West Van Buren Street, Chicago, Illinois 60607

Library of Congress Cataloging in Publication Data
Grant, Matthew G.
   Francis Marion—Swamp Fox.
                    (Gallery of great Americans)
   SUMMARY: A brief biography of the southern plantation owner whose knowledge of the swamps helped keep the Revolution alive in the South.
   1. Marion, Francis, 1732-1795—Juvenile literature. [1. Marion, Francis, 1732-1795. 2. United States—History—Revolution—Biography] I. Title. E207.M3G72 973.3'092'4 [B] [92] 73-10061
ISBN 0-87191-257-0

CONTENTS

IN OLD SOUTH CAROLINA   7

REVOLUTION BEGINS   14

WAR IN THE SWAMPS   19

VICTORY FOR THE FOX   27

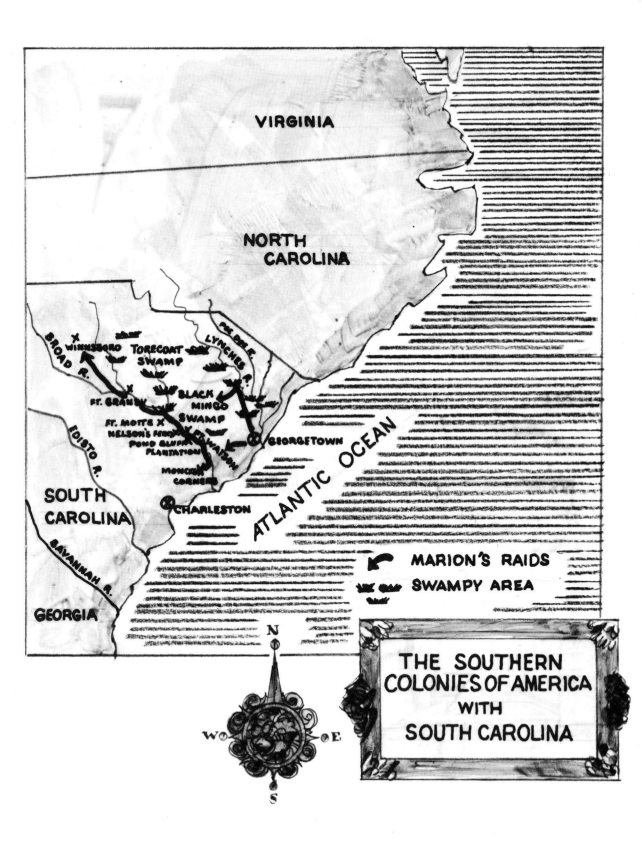

IN OLD SOUTH CAROLINA

In 1732, a sixth child was born to the Marion family of Goatfield Plantation. He was so tiny that he did not seem likely to live. "Hardly bigger than a lobster," his father said. "We'll call him Francis."

Francis was often sick, and he never grew as much as the other children. But he was a quick-witted boy, full of spirit as a bantam rooster. Often he would go off into the swamps that lay around the plantation. He would hunt or fish or just watch the birds and animals. And he never got lost.

When he was 15, Francis told his parents he wanted to become a sailor. He set off for the West Indies.

His schooner ran into a whale and sank. Francis and the other crewmen were cast adrift in an open boat for seven days. Some of the strong men died—but not weak Francis. They were finally rescued and Francis came home looking more healthy than ever. Danger seemed to agree with him!

He decided to give up the sea and help his parents with the plantation.

In those days, South Carolina was a royal colony of King George of England. But the French wanted to take over American lands. They urged the Indians to rise up and attack the settlers. Cherokee Indians fought the colonists in South Carolina.

Francis Marion joined the militia. He took part in the campaign that destroyed Cherokee villages and crops and forced the Indians to make a peace treaty.

After the Cherokee War, Francis Marion went back to farming. He prospered, and in 1773 he bought Pond Bluff, a large plantation on the Santee River. With the help of black slaves, he grew tobacco, corn, and other crops. And whenever he could, he slipped away to enjoy the mysterious peace of the swamps. He would glide along silently in a boat beneath the moss-hung cypress trees, fishing and thinking.

13

REVOLUTION BEGINS

For many years, American colonists had fretted under British rule. Most of the people of South Carolina—including Francis Marion— wanted liberty. In 1775 the colonists finally rebelled.

Francis Marion was elected an officer in the small colonial army. He and his men helped drive British troops out of Charleston, the most important seaport.

In June, 1776, British warships tried to re-take the city. Marion and his men fought them in the Battle of Fort Moultrie. Using captured cannons, the colonists drove the British ships away. On July 4, 1776, America declared its independence from Britain.

After a glorious start, the Revolutionary War in the South fizzled out. The British installed a powerful army at Savannah. The Americans did not dare attack it. For several years, the colonial troops had little to do. Many of them went to seed. But tough little Francis Marion did not let his men go to pieces. They did not have fancy uniforms or proper equipment. But he kept them alert and ready to fight.

WAR IN THE SWAMPS

American forces tried to take Savannah at last in 1779. But they were badly defeated. The survivors were put under the command of Francis Marion. He became the senior field officer in South Carolina.

The British had a new plan to crush the Americans. Lord Cornwallis, a British general, invaded South Carolina. He took Charleston. Francis Marion was able to escape. Most of the other American officers became prisoners of war.

An American Army under General Gates was badly defeated by Cornwallis at Camden, S.C. It looked like the Revolutionary War in the South was lost.

Francis Marion was still at large with about 30 black and white troops. He attacked the British and managed to free 150 American prisoners. Then he and his men fled into the Pee Dee River swamps.

The British chased him but their horses sank into the mud. "We'll never find that cursed Swamp Fox," said the British commander. Without knowing it, he had given Francis Marion a new name.

Marion became a guerilla fighter. He set up his camp on Snow's Island, deep in the swamp. From there, his small forces ranged out to attack British supply lines. His men suffered from hunger and from malaria. But they spread terror among the British army and those colonists still loyal to England. The people of South Carolina still hoped for liberty. A steady stream of men joined the little army in the swamp.

Cornwallis counted on loyal colonists
helping his army. A large loyalist force gath-
ered and marched to join him. But they were
met by Americans and defeated at the Battle
of King's Mountain in October, 1780. The
British lost their advantage.

Now General Nathanael Greene com-
manded American forces in the South. He
ordered Marion to attack Georgetown, on the
coast.

Marion had two forces. He ordered Colonel "Light-Horse" Harry Lee to attack with cavalry. The Swamp Fox himself brought another force down the Pee Dee in boats. They struck the British savagely. But without heavy guns, they could not break the walls of the fort at Georgetown. But Marion's partial success prevented British troops from leaving Georgetown. They could not join General Cornwallis up North.

VICTORY FOR THE FOX

Part of Cornwallis' army suffered a great defeat at Cowpens. The British then chased the American army into North Carolina, where Cornwallis fought Greene at Guilford Courthouse in March, 1781.

The Swamp Fox was ordered to cut British supply lines in the South. He also attacked British and loyalist troops still in South Carolina. Marion had only a small, poorly armed force, but he did a great amount of damage. He took Fort Watson. Then he took Fort Motte by means of fire arrows! On May 29, 1781, he marched into Georgetown and took it. The British had fled when they heard he was coming.

The Revolutionary War swiftly drew to a close. In Virginia, Washington's army closed in on Cornwallis.

In South Carolina, Marion and General Greene defeated the last large British force at the Battle of Eutaw Springs. This occured in August. By October, Cornwallis had surrendered to the Americans after the Battle of Yorktown. The Swamp Fox could hardly believe that peace had come at last.

In 1782, Francis Marion went home to Pond Bluff. It had been damaged during the war, but he soon had it repaired. He married his cousin, Mary Videau.

Many honors were given to him. He served in the South Carolina senate and finally saw South Carolina become the eighth state of the Union in 1788. His last years, until his death in 1795, were spent in the peaceful country he had loved.

★ ★

GALLERY OF GREAT AMERICANS SERIES

★ ★

INDIANS OF AMERICA
- GERONIMO
- CRAZY HORSE
- CHIEF JOSEPH
- PONTIAC
- SQUANTO
- OSCEOLA

EXPLORERS OF AMERICA
- COLUMBUS
- LEIF ERICSON
- DeSOTO
- LEWIS AND CLARK
- CHAMPLAIN
- CORONADO

FRONTIERSMEN OF AMERICA
- DANIEL BOONE
- BUFFALO BILL
- JIM BRIDGER
- FRANCIS MARION
- DAVY CROCKETT
- KIT CARSON

WAR HEROES OF AMERICA
- JOHN PAUL JONES
- PAUL REVERE
- ROBERT E. LEE
- ULYSSES S. GRANT
- SAM HOUSTON
- LAFAYETTE

WOMEN OF AMERICA
- CLARA BARTON
- JANE ADDAMS
- ELIZABETH BLACKWELL
- HARRIET TUBMAN
- SUSAN B. ANTHONY
- DOLLEY MADISON

★ ★